THE GREAT RESCUE

THE GREAT
RESCUE

—

UNDERSTANDING THE SAVING
WORK OF CHRIST

R.C. Sproul

 LIGONIER MINISTRIES

The Great Rescue
© 2024 by the R.C. Sproul Trust

This work is an abridgement of the work originally published in the
United States under the title:
Saved from What? by R.C. Sproul
© 2021 by the R.C. Sproul Trust

Published by Ligonier Ministries
421 Ligonier Court, Sanford, FL 32771
Ligonier.org

Printed in China
Amity Printing Company
0000924
First edition

ISBN 978-1-64289-616-9 (Paperback)
ISBN 978-1-64289-617-6 (ePub)

Cover design: Ligonier Creative
Interior typeset: Ligonier Editorial

Unless otherwise noted, Scripture quotations are from the ESV® Bible
(The Holy Bible, English Standard Version®), copyright © 2001 by
Crossway, a publishing ministry of Good News Publishers. Used by
permission. All rights reserved.

Library of Congress Control Number: 2024930873

CONTENTS

CHAPTER ONE

Saved from What?

"Are you saved?"

I recall vividly a time many years ago, in 1969, when I was asked this question.

These were the volatile days of the sixties—the era of the cultural revolution in America. I was a professor of theology at the Conwell School of Theology on the campus of Temple University in Philadelphia. One day after lunch, I began my trek across the plaza to my classroom. I was walking briskly to avoid being late. I was alone, minding my own business. Suddenly, apparently out of nowhere, a gentleman appeared in front of me, blocking my forward progress. He looked me in the eye and asked directly, "Are you saved?"

I wasn't quite sure how to respond to this intrusion. I uttered in response the first words that came into my mind: "Saved from what?" What I was thinking, but had the grace not to say, was, "I'm certainly not saved from strangers buttonholing me and asking me questions like yours." But when I said, "Saved from what?" I think the man who stopped me that day was as surprised by my question as I had been by his. He began to stammer and stutter. Obviously, he wasn't quite sure how to respond.

"Saved from what? Well, you know what I mean. You know, do you know Jesus?" Then he tried to give me a brief summary of the gospel.

This serendipitous encounter left an impression on me. I experienced real ambivalence. On the one hand, I was delighted in my soul that someone cared enough about me, even though I was a stranger, to stop me and ask about my salvation. But it was clear that, though this man had a zeal for salvation, he had little understanding of what salvation is. He was using Christian jargon. The words fell from his lips without being processed by his mind. As a result, his words were empty of content. Clearly, the man had a love for Christ and a concern for people. Few Christians have the courage to engage perfect strangers in evangelistic discussion. But sadly, he had little understanding of what he was so zealously trying to communicate.

Consider this profoundly shocking text that uniquely answers the question, "Saved from what?" The text reads:

> The great day of the Lord is near,
>> near and hastening fast;
> the sound of the day of the Lord is bitter;
>> the mighty man cries aloud there.
> A day wrath is that day,
>> a day of distress and anguish,
> a day of ruin and devastation,
>> a day of darkness and gloom,
> a day of clouds and thick darkness,
>> a day of trumpet blast and battle cry
> against the fortified cities
>> and against the lofty battlements.
>
> I will bring distress on mankind,
>> so that they shall walk like the blind,
>> because they have sinned against the Lord;

their blood shall be poured out like dust,
>   and their flesh like dung.
Neither their silver nor their gold
>   shall be able to deliver them
>   on the day of the wrath of the LORD.
In the fire of his jealousy,
>   all the earth shall be consumed;
for a full and sudden end
>   he will make of all the inhabitants of the earth.
(Zeph. 1:14–18)

If we read this text carefully, we will easily see that it has precious little "gospel" in it. The message is not "good news" but horrific news. It is so dire that one is not surprised when it is relegated to a hidden corner.

To be sure, the end of Zephaniah's book gives the divine promise of redemption. It ends on a high note, but not before stressing the dreadful exposure of the nation of Israel to the stark reality of divine judgment.

With a message so grim, what would even incline me to mention this text? Simply this: here in this seldom-heard passage we have the clearest biblical description in answer to the question, "Saved from what?" And when we're talking about salvation, we are talking about the concept that is *the central theme of all of sacred Scripture*— a concept that it is imperative to understand.

The Meaning of *Salvation*

When the Bible uses the word *salvation* or the verb *to save*, it doesn't necessarily refer to what we mean by the *doctrine* of salvation.

When Jesus healed people from illness during His earthly ministry, He sometimes said to them, "Your faith has saved you" (e.g., Luke 7:50). He was not speaking about eternal salvation but rather their rescue from a dreadful disease. At times in the Old Testament, when the people of Israel went into battle, God intervened on their behalf to save them from military defeat. That was rescue from a clear and present danger.

The Bible says that women will be "saved" through childbirth (1 Tim. 2:15). Paul also teaches the Corinthians that "the unbelieving husband is sanctified by the wife, and the unbelieving wife is sanctified by the husband" (1 Cor. 7:14). Does this mean that the New Testament teaches three ways of salvation: (1) having personal faith in Christ; (2) marrying somebody who has faith in Christ; and (3) for women, childbearing?

Obviously, we know that that is not what the Bible teaches. The Bible uses the term *salvation* in many ways. Not every time the word is used does it refer to our reconciliation with God. The common thread that is found in the many uses is that, at root, *salvation* means rescue or deliverance from some calamity or catastrophe.

Rescued from the Wrath to Come

Though the Bible refers to various types of salvation, when it speaks about salvation in the ultimate sense, it's speaking of the ultimate escape from the ultimate dire human condition. This brings us back to the question I asked the man in Philadelphia so many years ago: "Saved from what?" And the answer, the Scriptures tell us, is that we must be saved from the wrath that is to come.

God's wrath, as we're told in Romans 1, is revealed to the whole world, and the Bible makes it abundantly clear that there awaits a judgment. The greatest calamity that anybody can ever imagine is to be sentenced to hell. In his first epistle to the Thessalonians, Paul writes:

> For they themselves report concerning us the kind of reception we had among you, and how you turned to God from idols to serve the living and true God, and to wait for his Son from heaven, whom he raised from the dead, Jesus who delivers us from the wrath to come. (1 Thess. 1:9–10)

The ultimate salvation that any human being can ever experience is rescue from the wrath that is to come. Do we believe that there remains a wrath that is to come? I think the greatest point of unbelief in our culture and in our church today is an unbelief in the wrath of God and in His certain promise of judgment for the human race.

Christians get excited about the return of Jesus. Oh, happy day! Yes, it is a happy day for the saved, but for the unsaved the return of Jesus is the worst of all conceivable calamities. It is a day of desolation, as the prophet Zephaniah foretold. Near is the great day of the Lord. Near, coming very quickly, is that day of wrath, a day of trouble, of distress, destruction, desolation, darkness, gloom. And on the day of the Lord's wrath, all the earth will be devoured, for He will make a terrifying end to the inhabitants of this world.

Such a Great Salvation

When we think of escape, we think of some kind of deliverance from a dire and life-threatening situation—escaping from a kidnapper, or soldiers' being surrounded in battle and finding a way to retreat safely. That's an escape. But the most common idea with which we associate escape is imprisonment, particularly from those prisons that are the most notoriously inescapable, such as Alcatraz, Devil's Island, or the most dreadful of all French prisons, the Château d'If.

Do you remember the story? *The Count of Monte Cristo* tells the tale of Edmond Dantès, who was falsely accused of a crime, unjustly convicted, and then sent to the most dreaded prison, the Château d'If. He suffered for years in solitary confinement until one day, he met a co-prisoner who was an aged priest. The priest, who had been there for decades, had spent years trying to dig a tunnel to escape. But he had miscalculated the route and ended up entering into Dantès' chamber.

These two men started spending time together, and the old priest became Dantès' mentor. He taught him about science, philosophy, and theology. He also told Dantès about a map that led to a vast treasure hidden in the sea. One day, the old priest died, and through an extraordinary series of circumstances, his death led to the escape of Edmond Dantès from the Château d'If. He then found the vast treasure that financed the rest of his life with his nom de plume, the Count of Monte Cristo. What an escape story.

Maybe Alcatraz or Devil's Island could possibly be escaped, or even the Château d'If, but the one prison from which no one ever escapes is hell. There's no escape route. You can't dig under it. You can't climb over it. No guard can be bribed. The sentence cannot be ameliorated.

Consequently, the author of the book of Hebrews says, "How shall we escape if we neglect such a great salvation?" (2:3). This is a rhetorical question. And the answer to the question is simple. How shall we escape if we neglect such a great salvation? The answer is that we can't.

Salvation *of* and *from* the Lord

At the core of the biblical message of salvation is another concept often obscured in modern thought. Salvation is *of* the Lord. No human being has the resources, the power, the money, or the merit to save himself. The necessary power for rescue is not in us. It must come from God. Salvation is of the Lord because only the Lord can accomplish it.

However, when the Scriptures tell us that God saves us, that salvation is *of* the Lord, we tend to forget that salvation is also *from* the Lord. What do we need to be saved from? We need to be saved *from God*—not from kidney stones, not from hurricanes, not from military defeats.

What every human being needs to be saved *from* is God. The last thing in the world the impenitent sinner ever wants to meet on the other side of the grave is God. But the glory of the gospel is that the One from whom we need to be saved is the very One who saves us. God, in saving us, saves us from Himself.

Woe unto those who have no Savior on the day of wrath. The Bible says that on that day the unbeliever will scream to the mountains to fall upon him, to the hills to hide him (see Rev. 6:15–17). People will be looking for refuge from nature itself, crying: "Cover me! Give me a shield!" But there is only one Shield that can protect anyone from the wrath that is to come. It is the covering of the righteousness of Christ.

When we put our faith in Jesus, God cloaks us with the garments of Jesus, and the garments of Christ's righteousness are never, ever the target of God's wrath. He who flees to Jesus has peace with God, and there is no condemnation left.

Are you saved? That question is the most important issue any person will ever face.

When we consider even for a moment the frightening dimension of the unbridled outpouring of God's wrath, we tremble in our souls. When we consider that we deserve to be consumed by His fury and realize that His fury has instead consumed Jesus in our place, when we recognize the greatness of the peril, we then are able to see the greatness of the salvation that He has bestowed upon us. How shall we escape if we neglect so great a salvation?

The Shattered Self-Image

That we are shocked by the idea that we are saved *from* God reveals two crucial shortcomings in our understanding. We fail to understand who God is, and we fail to understand who we are. Our view of God is too low, and our view of mankind is too high. This was Isaiah's painful discovery when he got a glimpse of the unveiled holiness of God. In that encounter, Isaiah understood for the first time in his life who God is. It was also the first time he understood who he was. He cursed himself, crying:

"Woe is me, for I am lost; for I am a man of unclean lips, and I dwell in the midst of a people of unclean lips; for my eyes have seen the King, the LORD of hosts!" (Isa. 6:5).

Isaiah's discovery shattered his self-image. His vision of God made him come apart at the seams. And his experience was not unique in the biblical record. It seems that every person who encounters the living God in Scripture suddenly loses his self-composure and experiences a severe identity crisis. The ego is shattered into tiny pieces.

The Severity of Sin

The best self-image we can ever have is one that is accurate and true. The Bible makes it clear that we have value as creatures made in the image of God. We affirm the sanctity of human life because every person is made in God's image. But that image has been tarnished. It has been desecrated by sin.

As long as we discount the severity of our sin, we sense no fear of God. We are content with our performance as it is, deluding ourselves into believing that it is good enough to satisfy a holy God. This was precisely the condition of the rich young ruler who approached Jesus (Luke 18:18–23). When Jesus told him to obey the Ten Commandments, the rich young ruler replied, "All these I have kept from my youth" (v. 21).

At this point Jesus could have said: "I guess you weren't present when I preached the Sermon on the Mount and explained the full meaning of the law. If you understood the law as I have revealed it, you would realize that you haven't kept a single one of the commandments since you got out of your bed this morning." But Jesus didn't do that. Instead of telling the man that he had not kept the law, He *showed* him. In a sense, He took him straight to the first commandment about having no other gods. He instructed the fellow to sell his goods and give all to the poor. The man walked away sorrowfully, for he was very rich. He failed the test on the first commandment.

It is amazing how many "rich young rulers" there are in the world and the church today. Multitudes are secure that their destination is heaven because they think they have kept the Ten Commandments. They don't understand that by the works of the law no flesh will ever be justified in the sight of God (see Gal. 2:16). If we think we can make it into heaven by keeping the law, we are under the worst of all possible delusions. If we live by the law, we will die by the law.

God's Perfect Standard

Most of us harbor in our minds the feeling that all it's going to take to make us acceptable to God on the day of judgment is that we have tried, that we have done our best, and that we have been basically good. But the truth is, we are not even *close* to being good enough. I would say that the greatest and most frequent error that human beings make is the assumption that they are going to survive the judgment of a holy God on the basis of their own performance.

What would you say to God if He asked you, "Why should I let you into My heaven?" How would you answer that? How do you hope to stand before God? This calls attention to the problem of our fallenness. We think of our own sin as being merely on the surface, something that slightly mars the image of God, but we lack an accurate understanding of the degree and intensity of our alienation from God. All of us admit that no one is perfect. If I ask people if they are sinners, virtually all of them admit that they are. They often say, "Nobody's perfect." To be a sinner doesn't seem a serious matter to them. After all, "to err is human, to forgive, divine." The adage almost drips with the assumption that since God is divine, He is obligated to forgive us.

No Fear of God

Part of the reason that we never achieve the standard of righteousness or perfection that God requires of us, that none of us mirror or reflect His greatness, is that we don't understand what the standard is. We are so far removed in our thinking from God's holiness that we have become blinded to what sin is. We live in a culture where all of us do what is right in our own eyes, forgetting that it is the eye of God that determines what is good.

God made us, and He made us in His image. In making us in His image, He has built into our human makeup a capacity and a need to reverence our Creator. We know that God is worthy of our honor, our reverence, and our adoration. We know that it is our moral responsibility to give Him these things. But we have been disobedient for so long that we no longer even fear God. We laugh at Him. We think that He can't touch us or hurt us. That is how deep our sin goes. It is not just on the surface. It is not simply that we've missed the mark, that we are alienated from God, but that, in our natural state, we are actually enemies of God.

We arrive in this world fallen. Because of our fall in Adam, we are born with a corrupt nature. This is what is meant by *original sin*. Original sin is not the sin that Adam and Eve committed. It is the *result* of that first sin. Original sin has reference to our sinful condition, our sinful bent, our sinful inclination from which actual sin flows. In other words, *we sin because we are sinners.* We are not sinners because we sin. Since the fall of mankind, it is now the nature of human beings to be inclined and drawn to sinfulness. I sin because I am a sinner. David said, "I was brought forth in iniquity, and in sin my mother conceived me" (Ps. 51:5).

Poised to Be Shattered

We are sinners who cannot overcome our sin by ourselves. It is because of sin and its severity that we need a Savior. We need someone who will save us from the wrath to come.

Our best works are not good enough to meet God's standard of righteousness. Augustine defined our finest efforts as but "splendid vices." We flatter ourselves on our performance because we judge ourselves on a curve. We compare ourselves with others, and as long as there are people who seem more sinful than we are, we congratulate ourselves on our virtue. This is folly, as the Apostle Paul indicates:

Not that we dare to classify or compare ourselves with some of those who are commending themselves. But when they measure themselves by one another and compare themselves with one another, they are without understanding. But we will not boast beyond limits, but will boast only with regard to the area of influence God assigned to us (2 Cor. 10:12–13a)

Our damaged souls need more than earthly royalty to rescue us from the wrath of God. We need a greater remedy. We need an atonement. We need the cross.

CHAPTER TWO

Saved by What?

We have seen that the grand paradox or supreme irony of the Christian faith is that we are saved both *by* God and *from* God. The God of perfect holiness, who demands satisfaction for His justice and who will not wink at sin, has from all eternity decreed that He Himself should provide salvation to those very people who, by their sin, are exposed to His wrath and judgment.

The means *by* which God accomplishes this great salvation may be described as the most crucial aspect of the work of Christ. When we use the word *atonement*, we're speaking of the fact that God pays the price that He requires for us to be in a right relationship with Him, and He does that through His Son, Jesus Christ.

There are three dimensions of sin that necessitate atonement: (1) sin is a debt; (2) sin is an act of enmity; and (3) sin is a crime. To understand the debt aspect of sin, we must first understand the role of God as Creator and as Sovereign over the universe.

God's sovereignty is multifaceted. It concerns His absolute rule over nature, over history, over the affairs of mankind. Indeed, God's sovereignty focuses on His authority over all creation. Sovereignty involves authority. We see another word contained within the word *authority*. It is the word *author*. As the Author of all things, God has authority over all that He creates. As the Author of all things, He is thereby the Owner of all things. What He makes and owns He rules over. God intrinsically and absolutely has the right to impose obligations on His creation.

Sin as Debt

If God imposes obligations upon us that we fail to perform, then we incur debt. At this point, God becomes a creditor.

He is the One to whom we owe the debt. Jesus described us as debtors who cannot pay our debts. It is one thing to be in debt and be able to pay it by means of a debt-retirement program, whereby we pay off our debt a little bit at a time. But the indebtedness that we have with respect to obedience to God is impossible for us to pay back by installment plan or any other means. Why? What is the ethical obligation that God imposes upon us, His creatures? How righteous are we required to be? How moral are we called to be by divine mandate? We are required to be sinless—nothing less than moral perfection is required.

In our culture, we try to evade the consequences of our sin by declaring, "Everyone gets a second chance." We even promote this second chance to the level of merit by saying, "Everyone deserves a second chance." But who says that anybody deserves a second chance? Does justice require that everyone get a second chance? A second chance is grace. A second chance is mercy. Mercy and grace are things that are never deserved. They cannot be deserved. If they were deserved, they would be justice and not mercy. Deserved grace is simply not grace at all. To say that the creature deserves a second chance from the Creator is pure nonsense. Even if this nonsensical notion were true, what good would it do us? How long ago did we all use up our second chance?

Our problem is not that we are almost impeccable moral creatures with one tiny blemish marring a perfect record. Rather, the Scriptures describe us as woefully inadequate in terms of our obedience to God. It is not that we are merely tainted by an occasional peccadillo. Our sins are many and grave, so grave that payback is impossible.

How does Christ help me with my debt? What is the role that He carries out in His work as our Redeemer? The New Testament has a word for it. Christ is our "guarantor" (see Heb. 7:22). *Guarantor* is an economic term, just as *debt* is an economic term. When the Bible speaks this way, it borrows language from the business world. That Christ is our guarantor means that He is the One who cosigns our note. He backs up our indebtedness by taking upon Himself the obligation to pay what must be paid.

Sin as Enmity

We do not disobey God because we love Him deeply. We disobey God because we have an inborn hostility toward Him. The Bible says that we are by nature enemies of God. We have a natural antipathy in our fallenness toward God's reign over us. So with respect to enmity, God is the injured or offended party. It is not that God has manifested enmity toward us. We are the ones who have violated Him. God has never broken a promise. He has never violated a covenant. He has never sworn a vow to us that He failed to pay. He has never treated a human being unjustly. He has never violated me as a creature. He has never violated you. He has kept His side of the relationship perfectly. But we have violated Him. He is the injured party, not us.

The role that Christ plays in our redemption is that of Mediator. What does a mediator do? Where does the mediator stand? He stands in the middle, which is not a very popular place to be. In cases of estrangement, the mediator usually catches flak from both sides. It is like being an umpire or a referee between two combatants. The mediator often becomes a human lightning rod, attracting heat from both sides.

When we talk about mediation, we are concerned about *reconciliation*, a theme that is crucial to biblical Christianity. The purpose of mediation in an industrial contract dispute between labor and management is to accomplish reconciliation. The mediator is brought in to bring the two sides together where previous negotiations have failed. If there is no need for reconciliation, there is no need for a mediator. Reconciliation is needed only when estrangement has occurred—only when a relationship has been ruptured.

The Scriptures speak of such a ruptured personal relationship, a relationship that has been broken between two parties—God and man. There exists an estrangement between God and man, and reconciliation is necessary. It is into this situation of estrangement, of brokenness, that Christ comes as Mediator. He is our Supreme Mediator. Paul writes:

For there is one God, and there is one mediator

between God and men, the man Christ Jesus, who
gave himself as a ransom for all. (1 Tim. 2:5–6a)

The biblical revelation indicates that God is sorely
displeased with our offenses, and God the Father, as the
injured party, is angry with our sin.

Though many deny the reality of God's wrath, it is
taught so plainly in Scripture that others are loath to deny
it. But they often fall off the other side of the horse. They
substitute one distortion for the other. This error occurs
when God the Father is seen as being so consumed with
wrath toward us that it requires the benevolent and kind
intervention of the Son to bring the Father around—God
the Father is mad as a hornet at man, but God the Son
identifies so closely with our fallenness and our need that
in His love, patience, and compassion He sides with us and
acts as our Mediator to calm down the angry Father. This
view posits a tension or split within the Godhead itself, as
if the Father had one agenda and the Son persuaded Him
to change His mind. The Father is angry and intends to
mete out punishment and send everyone to hell, until the

Son intervenes to talk Him out of it. This view sees Jesus as saying: "Punish Me instead. Let Me stand in their place. Let Me not only mediate the discussion but absorb the anger. Pile it on Me, not on them. Let Me be the lightning rod, and You can take Your wrath out on Me."

However, when we think like this, we forget whose idea it was to provide a Mediator in the first place. The Mediator did not come on His own. God so loved the world that He "gave," that He "sent," His Son. Those two verbs we find in the Bible again and again and again. The Father sends the Son. The Father gives the Son for our redemption:

> For in him all the fullness of God was pleased to dwell, and through him to reconcile to himself all things, whether on earth or in heaven, making peace by the blood of his cross.
>
> And you, who once were alienated and hostile in mind, doing evil deeds, he has now reconciled in his body of flesh by his death, in order to present you holy and blameless and above reproach before him. (Col. 1:19–22)

Sin as Crime

The third dimension of sin is its criminal characteristic. Here God functions as the Governor and the Judge. God is ultimately the Judge in all matters of justice. He is the ultimate standard of righteousness. His own character is the ultimate standard of justice. He functions personally as the Judge of heaven and earth. Christ in the drama of the atonement does not function as the Judge. He is elevated to the role of Judge at His ascension, however, and that is significant. By contrast, in His descent to this world, Christ comes under judgment, and His role here is as priest-victim. He comes to be judged in our behalf.

When I sin against God, Jesus pays the price for my indebtedness. In order for that payment to be accepted, the Judge, who is at the same time the injured party, must decide and decree that He will accept that payment in my behalf. If I owed God the death penalty because I sinned against Him, and Jesus said, "I will die for him," and laid down His life for me, would God be under any obligation to accept that payment? None whatsoever.

There first must be a decision by the Governor of the universe that He will accept a substitutionary payment in order for my crime to be covered. The decision of God the Father to do so is one of sheer grace.

God demands that justice be done. The price must be paid. The debt will be paid in full, in both a pecuniary sense and a penal sense. He judges our crime. Our crime is punished. The debt is paid. God does not negotiate His justice. Yet at the same time, our debt and the punishment for our crime are paid by a substitute. Thus, the cross shows both perfect justice and perfect mercy. Take away the substitution and you take away the grace of God. Take away the cross and you take away the justice and righteousness of God. In this transaction we see what Paul meant when he said that God is "just and the justifier of the one who has faith in Jesus" (Rom. 3:26).

Christ Our Ransom

When Jesus had to state succinctly, poignantly, and graphically what His ministry was about so that His disciples would understand, He framed His mission in terms of giving His life as a ransom:

> "You know that those who are considered rulers of the Gentiles lord it over them, and their great ones exercise authority over them. But it shall not be so among you. But whoever would be great among you must be your servant, and whoever would be first among you must be slave of all. For even the Son of Man came not to be served but to serve, and to give his life as a ransom for many." (Mark 10:42–45)

In the ancient world, the idea of *ransom* functioned very much like the idea of *ransom* in our own language. When we think of ransom, we think of kidnapping, where someone abducts a person and then demands payment for the release of the person who is being held hostage. The kidnappers expect a monetary payment. That is similar to how the concept functioned in antiquity. The ransom was a price paid to release a slave from bondage. Or hostages held in military conflicts could be purchased and set free by a ransom.

When the Bible speaks of ransom, the ransom is paid not to a criminal but to the One who is owed the price for redemption—the One who is the offended party, the injured party in the whole process of sin. And who is that? Again, it is God the Father. Jesus, as the Servant, offers Himself in payment to the Father for us.

Substitution and Satisfaction

The fact that the New Testament writers understood Jesus' ministry on the cross in terms of a ransom demands an understanding of substitution and satisfaction. In a ransom situation, a price is paid by someone other than the individual for whom it is being paid. The demand for the ransom is being satisfied by a substitute. Jesus says, "I lay down my life for the sheep" (John 10:15)—"in behalf of" the sheep. "I give My life in behalf of the many." In behalf of, in behalf of, in behalf of—this is the recurring, resounding refrain of Jesus' own self-understanding.

When Jesus explained His agenda, He was talking in the first person and communicating to His hearers what

His mission was. At the center of His teaching was this: He was not working to save Himself; He was offering Himself as a substitute in our behalf.

Expiation and Propitiation

The work of Christ was done to placate the wrath of God. This idea of placating the wrath of God has done little to placate the wrath of modern theologians. Modern theologians have become wrathful about the idea of placating the wrath of God! They think that it is beneath the dignity of God that He has to be placated—that we have to do something to soothe Him or to appease Him. I grant that we need to be very careful in how we understand the wrath of God and placation. But let me remind you that the concept of placating the wrath of God has to do not with a peripheral, tangential point of theology but with the very essence of salvation.

When we talk about salvation biblically, we have to remember from what ultimately we are saved. We are saved from the wrath that is to come, the wrath of God.

We cannot understand either the mission of Christ or His cross apart from Jesus' own teaching about judgment. He constantly warned people that someday the whole world was coming into judgment. What is done in corners and in secret will be made manifest. Jesus said that every idle word will come into the judgment. His was a "crisis" theology. The Greek word *krisis* means "judgment." The crisis of which Jesus preached was the crisis of an impending judgment of the world, at which point God is going to pour out His wrath against the unredeemed, the ungodly, and the impenitent. The only hope of escape from the wrath of God is to be covered by the atonement of Christ. The supreme achievement of the cross is that Christ has placated the wrath of God, which would burn against me were I not covered by His sacrifice.

The Atonement and Justification

How does the cross of Christ relate to us? We are now finished with the objective question of what happened on the cross, and we turn to the subjective question of how the benefit of Christ's work is appropriated to us. What good is it for us that Christ died on the cross? How does that relate to us? What actually happened on the cross? Again, we're talking about the atonement as it relates to the concept of justification. This word *justification* is one of those long, ponderous theological terms that we find in the Bible. But it is at the very heart of the gospel. Sadly, many people in the church have trouble defining the term *justification*.

Let us remember that the need for an atonement is related to the problem of human sin and the character of God—God's holiness and justice. We can illustrate the problem with the following circles.

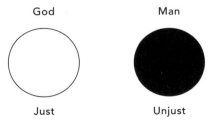

The problem we face is this: God is just, and we are unjust. How are we going to reconcile this conflict between a just and holy God and a fallen, unjust, sinful human being?

To work with this imagery for a minute, let us suppose that the circle on the right represents the character of mankind. If man sins, that sin puts a blemish of sorts, a moral blemish, on the character of fallen man. If he commits another sin, and sin penetrates more deeply into his life, we might add another dot. The issue then becomes, How much of the circle should be shaded when we are judged by the standard of God's perfection? Human corruption is total. It is not that sin touches merely the edges of our lives. It penetrates to the core of our being. Nor is there an island of righteousness preserved in our soul where sin has not reached. Rather, the corruption of sin reaches the whole person.

No One Is Righteous

To take it further, when the Apostle Paul elaborated on this fallen human condition, he said, "None is righteous, no, not one; . . . no one does good" (Rom. 3:10, 12). That is a radical statement. He was saying that fallen man never does a single good deed. That flies in the face of our experience. We look around us, and we see all kinds of folks who are not Christians doing things that we would applaud for their virtue. We see acts of self-sacrificial heroism, kindness, and charity, for example, among those who are not Christian. John Calvin called this *civil righteousness*.

The reason we struggle with the biblical claim that no one does good is that our perspective of the good differs from that of Scripture. First, we must consider the measuring rod of the law, which is God's measurement of the external performance of human beings. For example, if God says that we are not allowed to steal, and we go our whole lives without ever stealing anything, we have kept the law externally. At least in this outward performance, our record is clear.

But in addition to the external measuring rod, there is also the consideration of the heart, the internal motivation for our behavior. We judge by outward appearance. God looks on the heart. From a biblical perspective, to do a good deed in the fullest sense of the word requires not only that the deed conform outwardly to the standards of God's law but that it proceed from a heart that loves Him and wants to honor Him. We remember the great commandment: "You shall love the Lord your God with all your heart" (Matt. 22:37). Let's just stop there for a second. Is there anybody in this world who has loved God with all of his heart for even the last five minutes? No. Nobody has loved God with all of his heart since being born, nor have we loved Him with all of our mind or strength.

I know that one of the things I will be accountable for on judgment day is the way in which I have failed in the pursuit of the knowledge of God. Many times I have been lazy and slothful and too bored to apply myself to the fullest possible measure of knowing God. I have not loved God with all of my mind. If I loved God with all of my mind, there would never be an impure thought in my head. But that's not the way my head works.

If we considered human performance from God's perspective, we would see why Paul came to that seemingly radical conclusion that there is none righteous, no, not one, that there is none who does good. In the full sense of the word, there is no goodness found in fallen people. Even in our finest works there is a taint of sin mixed in. I have never in my life done an act of charity, an act of sacrifice, or an act of heroism out of a heart that loved God completely or out of a mind that loved God completely. Externally, all kinds of virtuous acts are going on among both believers and unbelievers. But God considers both the external and the internal. Under that tight norm of judgment, we're in trouble. Because of our sin, our circle becomes completely shaded.

Man

How Can an Unjust Person Be Made Righteous?

How is an unjust person going to stand in the presence of God? How can the unjust person be justified? How can the unjust person be made just? Can he start all over again? Can he erase his sin? He cannot. Once a person sins, it is impossible to ever be perfect. He has already lost his perfection by his initial sin. We have a serious problem here. Some may say that the problem is not severe because God in His kindness will overlook it. God could do this if He were willing to negotiate His own righteousness or sacrifice His own justice. But then the Judge of all the earth would not be doing what is right. A judge who does not punish evil is neither just nor good.

Here is where mediation is required. It is at this point that Christ comes to act as our Mediator. When we consider our redemption, we tend to think that salvation comes to us simply through the death of Christ. While we are focusing our attention on the death of Christ, it is very easy to overlook something of absolutely crucial significance for the atonement to have any value at all. If I ask a child, "What did Jesus do for you?" the response will be, "Jesus died for my sins." But if that is all Jesus did, then why didn't He just come down from heaven at age thirty and go straight to the cross? The point of the atonement is that a *just* man died for the unjust. But to qualify to be the Redeemer, to qualify to be the Savior, Jesus first had to live a perfect life. He had to live a life of perfect obedience. He had to acquire merit at the bar of justice. What is often overlooked in our justification is that there is a double transaction that takes place.

Justification: A Double Transaction

Let us illustrate that double transaction. In the circle below representing Jesus, there are no blemishes. He is the One for whom John the Baptist sang the *Agnus Dei*, "Behold, the Lamb of God, who takes away the sin of the world!" (John 1:29). The Lamb of God is the Lamb without blemish. Jesus Himself challenged His enemies to convict Him of sin. None were able to do so.

Even at Jesus' trial, Pontius Pilate announced that he could find no fault in Him.

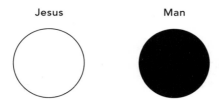

Jesus   Man

Jesus never flinched from obeying the law in its fullness. In Him there was no shadow of turning, no blemish, no sin. His "food" was to do the will of the Father (John 4:34). Zeal for His Father's house consumed Him (2:17). His passion in life was obedience to the Father. "I do nothing on My own authority, but only what the Father tells Me to do. I and the Father are one." It was for these claims that His enemies picked up rocks to attack Him.

In the drama of justification we have one unjust party and two just parties. We have a just God, and we have a just Mediator, who is altogether holy. The justification of which the New Testament speaks we call *forensic* justification. Forensics has to do with formal acts of authoritative, legal declaration. Forensic justification means that a person is declared to be just at the tribunal of God. The justification takes place ultimately when the supreme Judge of heaven and earth says, "You are just."

The question is, On what possible grounds could God ever say to us, "You are just," when in fact we are not just? Again, how can an unjust person be justified? We find the answer in the biblical concept of *imputation*. We see it in the imagery of the Lamb of God's bearing our sins just as the Old Testament scapegoat bore the sins of the people. As the priest put his hands on the goat, he was symbolically transferring or imputing the sins of the people to the animal.

Justification: Our Sin Transferred to Christ

In our justification, a double transfer takes place. First the weight of our guilt is transferred to Christ. Christ willingly takes upon Himself all of our sin. Once our sin is imputed to Christ, God sees Him as a mass of corruption. He sees a mass of sinfulness. Because the sin now has been transferred to Jesus' account, He is counted or reckoned guilty in our place.

But if this transfer were all that happened, if the imputation were a one-dimensional transaction, we would never be justified. If Jesus were to take on His back all of the sins that I have ever committed and bear the punishment for me, that would not get me into the kingdom of God. All that would do is to keep me out of hell. I would still not be just. I would be innocent but still not just in a positive sense. I would have no righteousness of which to speak. Remember, it is not simply innocence that gets us into the kingdom of God. It is righteousness. Unless our righteousness exceeds that of the scribes and Pharisees, we will never enter the kingdom of heaven (see Matt. 5:20). If the only thing that occurred in salvation were the removal of my guilt, I would still have no merit.

Justification: Christ's Righteousness Transferred to Us

So there is a double transfer. Not only is the sin of mankind imputed to Christ, but His righteousness is transferred to our account. In God's sight, our circle is now clean.

When God declares me just, He is not lying. This is no mere legal fiction.

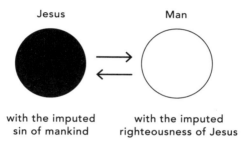

Jesus

Man

with the imputed
sin of mankind

with the imputed
righteousness of Jesus

If the imputation were fictional, then God's declaration would be a legal fiction. It would be a lie and a blemish on the character of God. But the point of the gospel is that the imputation is real. God really did lay my sins on Christ, and God actually did transfer Christ's righteousness to me. There is a genuine union for those who are in Christ. We truly possess the righteousness of Jesus Christ by imputation. Christ is our righteousness. That's why He is our Savior: not merely because He died but because He lived. Without His meritorious life, the atonement would have no value. Without His obedience, His suffering on the cross would be merely a tragedy. We must have the double transfer, by which God declares us just.

When we consider this double imputation, we see the essence of our salvation in a phrase made famous by Martin Luther: *simul justus et peccator*. *Simul* is the Latin word from which we get the English word *simultaneous*. It means "at the same time." *Justus* is the word for "just" or "righteous." *Et* means "and." *Peccator* is the Latin word for "sinner." So *simul justus et peccator* means "at the same time just and sinner." This is the glory of the doctrine of justification by faith alone. The person who is in Christ is at the very same instant both just and a sinner. That's good news, for if I had to wait until there was no sin in me to get into the kingdom of God, I would surely never make it.

Justification: By Christ Alone

The whole point of the gospel is that the minute I embrace Jesus Christ, all that Christ has done is applied to me. All that He is becomes mine, including His righteousness.

Luther's phrase "at the same time just and sinner" means that, at the very instant that I believe, I am just by virtue of the imputation of Christ's righteousness. It is Christ's righteousness that makes me just. His death has taken care of the punishment I deserve. His life has made possible my eternal reward. There it is. My justice is all tied up in Christ. And yet at the same time, in and of myself I am a sinner. It is sinners who are saved by the atonement. That is the glory of the gospel and of the cross. The Bible tells us that the only way we can have the righteousness and the merit of Christ transferred to our account is by faith. We cannot earn it. We cannot deserve it. We cannot merit it. We can only trust in it and cling to it.

Justification by faith alone means very simply this. Justification is by Christ alone. It is by His merit, His righteousness, His life, His death that we can stand in the presence of a holy God. Without Christ, we are without hope because all we can ever offer to God is our "unjustness."

No wonder the author of Hebrews asked, "How shall we escape if we neglect such a great salvation?" (2:3). That is a rhetorical question. The answer to the question is obvious. How will we escape? We will not. We cannot, because it is impossible for an unjust person to survive in the presence of a just God. We need to be justified. We're going to seek justification either through our own righteousness or through what the Reformers called a *foreign righteousness*. And the only foreign righteousness available for us is the righteousness of Christ.

CHAPTER THREE

Saved for What?

It is a precious thing to watch a saint die. The death of saints is sweet in the eyes of God. We get all sorts of advice on how to live but few lessons on how to die. We have a tendency to forget that the goal of our whole lives points beyond the grave. As we pass through this life, we often let our gaze wander away from our goal. We cling tenaciously to this life as if it were better than what lies ahead. Our attitude is rarely that expressed by Paul when he wrote:

> For I know that through your prayers and the help of the Spirit of Jesus Christ this will turn out for my

deliverance, as it is my eager expectation and hope that I will not be at all ashamed, but that with full courage now as always Christ will be honored in my body, whether by life or by death. For to me to live is Christ, and to die is gain. If I am to live in the flesh, that means fruitful labor for me. Yet which I shall choose I cannot tell. I am hard pressed between the two. My desire is to depart and be with Christ, for that is far better. But to remain in the flesh is more necessary on your account. (Phil. 1:19–24)

Paul does not denigrate this life. This life is good, and we seek to enjoy it to the fullest. This is my Father's world, and I am not to despise it. In this world I do not experience the absence of God, for Christ sent His Holy Spirit to be His presence for us here. But there is a new dimension to the presence of Christ when we pass through the veil. Then we enter directly into His *immediate* presence.

Again we notice that Paul is not in a quandary simply between living and dying. Rather, it is between leaving and staying. He doesn't want to leave just to be rid of this world and its afflictions. He is not looking for an escape hatch. He wants to depart so that he can be with Christ. That is his deepest desire.

Entering into the Presence of Christ

The promise of entering into Christ's presence came initially from the lips of Jesus Himself. In His Upper Room Discourse to His disciples, Jesus said:

> "Let not your hearts be troubled. Believe in God; believe also in me. In my Father's house are many rooms. If it were not so, would I have told you that I go to prepare a place for you? And if I go and prepare a place for you, I will come again and will take you to myself, that where I am you may be also. And you know the way to where I am going." (John 14:1–4)

Jesus' command to His friends was that they not allow their hearts to be troubled. He spoke of the many rooms in His Father's house. As Jesus was about to leave His friends, He assured them that He was going ahead of them to make preparations for the time they would rejoin Him. He promised that where He was, they would be too.

Adopted in Christ

Heaven, our destination, is inseparably linked to our adoption in Christ. We are promised rooms in our Father's house because we have been adopted into our Father's family. As His family members, we become His heirs. Paul describes our adoption in Romans 8:14–18:

> For all who are led by the Spirit of God are sons of God. For you did not receive the spirit of slavery to fall back into fear, but you have received the Spirit of adoption as sons, by whom we cry, "Abba! Father!" The Spirit himself bears witness with our spirit that we are children of God, and if children, then heirs—heirs of God and fellow heirs with Christ, provided we suffer with him in order that we may also be glorified with him.

For I consider that the sufferings of this present time are not worth comparing with the glory that is to be revealed to us.

The linkage between our adoption in Christ and our future blessedness in heaven is declared in 1 John 3:1–3:

Behold what manner of love the Father has bestowed on us, that we should be called children of God! Therefore the world does not know us, because it did not know Him. Beloved, now we are children of God; and it has not yet been revealed what we shall be, but we know that when He is revealed, we shall be like Him, for we shall see Him as He is. And everyone who has this hope in Him purifies himself, just as He is pure. (NKJV)

John calls attention to the end or purpose for which we are made. He declares our highest point of glory—the very acme of our salvation. He begins with the word "Behold." It is a summons to pay close attention. It is a call to stop and rivet our attention on what is about to come.

John is writing to the church when he says, "Look . . . behold what manner of love . . ." He stops us in our tracks. He asks us to consider the specific type or category of love that is revealed in our salvation. We could take the category of *love* and divide it into numerous different species: there is puppy love, erotic love, romantic love . . . and there is spiritual love. We can examine all the varieties of love, but John says: "Wait a minute. What kind of love is this, that we should be called the children of God?"

John utters his astonishment at the adopting love of God: "Behold what manner of love the Father has bestowed on us, that we should be called children of God!" (1 John 3:1). We don't have a category for that kind of love. There is nothing common or ordinary about it.

The Astonishing Reality of Our Adoption

It seems that in our day we have been inoculated against such amazement. We have been immunized to the astonishing reality of our adoption. We have been told over and over that we are all God's children. We assume that God is our Father by nature.

By no means! The Bible asserts that by nature we are children of wrath. There is no universal fatherhood of God or universal brotherhood of man. The Bible speaks of a universal *neighborhood*. All people are my neighbors, and I am to treat them with Christian love. But not all people are my brothers and sisters. That kinship comes only by adoption. Jesus is God's only natural Son. All others enter His family through adoption in Christ.

The assumptions of people living in the first century were different from ours. Being children of God was not assumed. Indeed, it was a radical idea. For John, it was incredible that the Lord God omnipotent would look at us and call us family.

God's Immeasurable Love

I can think of no reason why any of us are in the family of God, other than that the Father has been determined from the foundation of the world that His Son would "see the labor of His soul, and be satisfied" (Isa. 53:11, NKJV). We are, as Christ indicates in John 17, the ones that the Father has given to the Son. It is because of the immeasurable love that the Father has for His Son that we are called the children of God. Because the Father loves our older brother, we have been adopted into His family and have been seated at His table.

We must never take this unspeakable privilege for granted. Every time we pray and address God as "Father," we should think of the extraordinary love that makes this filial address possible. John says, "Behold what manner of love the Father has bestowed on us, that we should be called children of God! Therefore the world does not know us, because it did not know Him" (1 John 3:1).

"We Shall See Him as He Is"

I don't think I have ever in my life heard a sermon on the beatific vision, and I cannot fathom why. It is the ultimate prize, the ultimate goal for the Christian.

The word *beatific* comes from the same root from which we get the word *beatitude*. Thus, the beatific vision is a vision of supreme blessedness, the blessedness we will experience when we see God face to face.

John continues:

> Now we are children of God; and it has not yet been revealed what we shall be, but we know that when He is revealed, we shall be like Him, for we shall see Him as He is. And everyone who has this hope in Him purifies himself, just as He is pure. (1 John 3:2–3, NKJV)

John tells us that we shall see God as He is (in the Latin, *in se est*). The idea here is that we are going to see God, not the way He would appear in a cloud of shekinah glory, not in a burning bush, not in the pillar of smoke of the Old Testament, not by way of theophany, not by way of outward appearances. God is a spirit. We are going to see Him in His essence.

Imagine having an unmediated, direct apprehension of the very being of God. That is what the New Testament promises will occur at the end of the Christian's earthly life. We don't yet know what we're going to be. But we know this: we're going to be like Him, and we're going to see Him as He is.

Seeing the Pure Glory of God

The Bible tells us that the end of our sanctification will be our glorification, when all vestigial remnants of sin will be removed from our character. We will be pure. No more doubt. No more fear. No more error. No more pain. No more evil. All of these things will be gone forever. We will be like Christ, totally sanctified. We will see Him as He is in His unveiled splendor and glory. We will see something that will dwarf the vision that Isaiah had of the Holy One.

This is the destiny that God promises His people. This is the goal and purpose of our salvation. This is what we are saved *for*. We are saved *by* God, *from* God, *for* God. That is the full irony of the drama of salvation.

A New Heaven and a New Earth

Finally, we read of God's promise of a new heaven and a new earth, the promise of a new Jerusalem that will descend from heaven itself. This is the capstone of the revelation that John received while exiled on the isle of Patmos:

> Then I saw a new heaven and a new earth, for the first heaven and the first earth had passed away, and the sea was no more. And I saw the holy city, new Jerusalem, coming down out of heaven from God, prepared as a bride adorned for her husband. And I heard a loud voice from the throne saying, "Behold, the dwelling place of God is with man. He will dwell with them, and they will be his people, and God himself will be with them as their God. He will wipe away every tear from their eyes, and death shall be no more, neither shall there be mourning, nor crying, nor pain anymore, for the former things have passed away."
>
> And he who was seated on the throne said, "Behold, I am making all things new." Also he said,

"Write this down, for these words are trustworthy and true." And he said to me, "It is done! I am the Alpha and the Omega, the beginning and the end. To the thirsty I will give from the spring of the water of life without payment. The one who conquers will have this heritage, and I will be his God and he will be my son." (Rev. 21:1–7)

John describes in terms of streets of gold, gates of pearls, and walls adorned with precious stones the heavenly city to which we are given title by Christ. He describes a city of such magnificent beauty that it makes the most majestic human constructions of this world appear as blighted slums in contrast.

This city has no church. No spires or steeples mark its skyline. No temple is present because in this place none is needed:

And I saw no temple in the city, for its temple is the Lord God the Almighty and the Lamb. And the city has no need of sun or moon to shine on it, for the glory of God gives it light, and its lamp is the Lamb. By its light will the nations walk, and the kings of the earth will bring their glory into it, and its gates will never be shut by day—and there will be no night there. They will bring into it the glory and the honor of the nations. (Rev. 21:22–26)

Rescued for Glory

Finally, in the last chapter of the Bible, John describes a pure river—a river of the water of life, clear as crystal. It is in this majestic setting that our beatific vision will take place. It is here that the ultimate chapter of our salvation will be written:

Then the angel showed me the river of the water of life, bright as crystal, flowing from the throne of God and of the Lamb through the middle of the street of the city; also, on either side of the river, the tree of life with its twelve kinds of fruit, yielding its fruit each month. The leaves of the tree were for the healing of the nations. No longer will there be anything accursed, but the throne of God and of the Lamb will be in it, and his servants will worship him. They will see his face, and his name will be on their foreheads. And night will be no more. They will need no light of lamp or sun, for the Lord God will be their light, and they will reign forever and ever. (Rev. 22:1–5)

How, then, "shall we escape if we neglect such a great salvation" (Heb. 2:3)? It is a salvation that is *by* God, *from* God, and *for* God, to whom belongs all glory.

About the Author

Dr. R.C. Sproul was founder of Ligonier Ministries, first minister of preaching and teaching at Saint Andrew's Chapel in Sanford, Fla., first president of Reformation Bible College, executive editor of *Tabletalk* magazine, and general editor of the *Reformation Study Bible*. His radio program, *Renewing Your Mind*, is still broadcast daily on hundreds of radio stations around the world and can also be heard online. He was author of more than one hundred books, including *The Holiness of God*, *Chosen by God*, and *Everyone's a Theologian*. He was recognized throughout the world for his articulate defense of the inerrancy of Scripture and the need for God's people to stand with conviction upon His Word.